Frontier Surgeons

Frontier Surgeons

A Story about the Mayo Brothers

by Emily Crofford
illustrations by Karen Ritz

A Carolrhoda Creative Minds Book

Carolrhoda Books, Inc./Minneapolis

To editor Lisa Kee

LIBRARY OF CONGRESS CATALOGING-IN-PUBLICATION DATA

Crofford, Emily.
    Frontier surgeons : a story about the Mayo brothers / by
Emily Crofford ; illustrations by Karen Ritz.
        p.   cm.—(A Carolrhoda creative minds book)
    Summary: A biography of the two doctor brothers whose Minnesota
clinic became world-famous.
    ISBN 0-87614-381-8
    1. Mayo, William James, 1861-1939—Juvenile literature. 2. Mayo,
Charles Horace, 1865-1939—Juvenile literature. 3. Physicians—
United States—Biography. [1. Mayo, William James, 1861-1939.
2. Mayo, Charles Horace, 1865-1939. 3. Physicians.] I. Ritz,
Karen, ill. II. Title. III. Series.
R154.M33.C67   1989
610'.92'273—dc20
[B]   89-33601
                                                                    CIP
                                                                     AC

Manufactured in the United States of America

        3   4   5   6   7   8   9   10   99   98   97   96   95   94   93   92   91

Table of Contents

Chapter One

At the Rochester, Minnesota, train station, eleven-year-old Will Mayo tugged on the reins to stop the horses. Will's brother, Charlie, who was seven years old, and their big sister Gertrude sat beside him in the buggy. They had come to meet their father, who had spent most of the year 1872 studying at Bellevue Hospital in New York City.

The train pulled in, and after excited greetings, Dr. Mayo said he needed to stop by the office on the way home. That pleased Will and Charlie. They had washed the office windows and scrubbed the floors for his homecoming.

Dr. Mayo looked around with approval when they reached the office. "You did a fine job," he said. As they left to go home, Dr. Mayo picked up his microscope.

Will looked at Charlie. Why was Father taking the microscope with him?

Charlie shrugged. He didn't understand either. Maybe Father wanted to look at the germs he had brought home with him. Charlie had heard a lot of talk about his father's having gone away to learn more about germs.

At home, Mrs. Mayo and Phoebe, the sister between Will and Gertrude, had prepared a special breakfast. After breakfast, Dr. Mayo set the old microscope on the table and took out a folder with a picture of a streamlined, modern micro-scope. He would like to buy it, he told Mrs. Mayo, but it was very expensive. And the year of study in New York had been very costly.

Will understood that it would be a sacrifice, but he knew what the final decision would be. His mother had a telescope on the roof. She taught the children about stars the same way Dr. Mayo taught them about medicine. She gave botany lessons when they helped her weed the garden. And shelves of books lined the living room. Learning was important in their lives. Important enough to make sacrifices for.

After much discussion, Dr. and Mrs. Mayo decided to mortgage the house to pay for the new microscope and Dr. Mayo's studies in New York. Dr. Mayo told Will and Charlie that since Rochester was such a long way from Germany, where the microscope was made, it would probably take a year for it to arrive.

Will and Charlie looked forward to studying specimens with the new microscope, but in the meantime, they were busy with chores and school.

At school, tall, strong Will, with his pride and his quick temper, had vowed to beat up any boy who bothered his little brother. Charlie was not strong enough to wrestle and fight. It was soon apparent, though, that Charlie didn't need anybody to take care of him. His easygoing manner and his sense of humor won him many friends.

When he wasn't in school, Will liked most of all to ride his bay pony, Tony. His father had given Tony to him on his eighth birthday, and Will raced Tony through the streets of Rochester.

Charlie didn't share Will's enthusiasm for horses. He was more interested in mechanical things. His family was always asking, "Charlie, can you fix this? Would you repair that?"

One of Will and Charlie's most boring chores was pumping water. They had to pump water for drinking, for the horses, and for washing dishes and clothes.

When he was thirteen, Charlie talked his parents into buying a small engine, which he rigged to the water pump. Will watched as Charlie started it up to see if it worked. They clapped and cheered as the water splashed into the bucket.

Even though they wouldn't have to pump water anymore, there was still plenty of work to do at home—and at their father's office. They swept and dusted the office, rolled bandages, mixed salves and poultices, and even helped their father with postmortems.

As county coroner, it was one of Dr. Mayo's duties to examine the body tissues of people who had died, to determine the cause of death. Postmortems also helped doctors learn more about diseases. And the more they learned about a disease, the more likely they were to find a way to treat it.

Dr. Mayo had begun to take Will along to autopsies when Will was so small that he had to sit on the dissection table to see what was going on. He sometimes held on to the corpse's hair to keep from falling off the table. By the time he reached his teens, Will was helping his father with postmortems. And when he was sixteen, his father left him alone with a corpse.

Chapter Two

Gusts of wind stirred the night as Will and his father went into the Bradley House, an abandoned hotel. They had to do an autopsy on the caretaker, an old man who had lived there alone. The man's job had been to see that hobos didn't camp in the building. No one knew why the caretaker had died.

The single lamp that provided light was low on kerosene. Soot blackened its glass chimney. Will looked around at the dark corners and wavering shadows. He listened to the shrieks and moans the wind made as it blew through broken windows. While he and his father worked on the cadaver, which lay on an old iron bed, the lamp almost went out twice.

When they had taken all the tissue samples they needed, Dr. Mayo looked at his pocket watch. "It's eleven o'clock," he said. "I have to look in on a patient. Finish up here, please, Will."

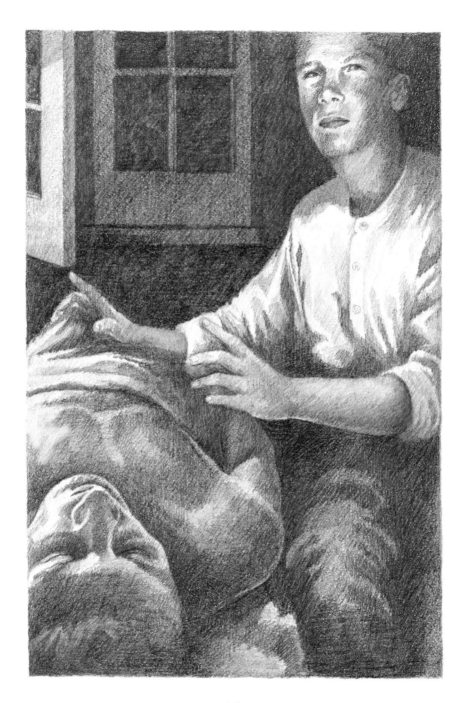

Will heard the carriage move away. His hand trembled as he sewed up the incisions. He was tucking the sheet around the corpse when he heard the chink, chink, chink of chains scraping against wood. The hair rose on the back of his neck; he grabbed the specimens and practically ran out the door.

Charlie laughed when Will told him about it the next day. They figured the "ghost" Will had heard was probably the chains that held the hotel sign scraping against the walls.

The boys also assisted their father with surgery, which generally meant amputation. If a person had a compound fracture, in which the broken bone punctures the skin, the injured limb was removed. Otherwise, infection would start at the puncture point, and since there was no way to stop it, the infection would spread through the body and kill the patient.

In addition to amputation, skin tumors were sometimes removed, but doctors didn't remove tumors from inside the body. Some doctors had tried cutting into the body, but since they didn't know how to deal with shock and infection in the 1870s, the attempts were generally unsuccessful.

After much study and observation in cities such

as New York and Chicago, Dr. Mayo began to do a particular operation that required cutting into the body. Called an ovariotomy, it involved the removal of a tumor from a woman's ovary. Many women were in misery from ovarian tumors, which sometimes weighed forty pounds. Few American doctors performed this operation, and Dr. Mayo was among the very first in Minnesota to do ovariotomies.

On a warm summer day in 1880, not long after Will's nineteenth birthday, Dr. Mayo told Will and Charlie that he planned to perform an ovariotomy the next day. "I need your help," he said.

Rochester didn't have a hospital. In fact, there were few hospitals anywhere in the country. Operations took place on the patient's kitchen table or living room sofa. This patient lived on a farm outside of Rochester.

The next morning, Will and Charlie dressed in their Sunday suits. Charlie stuck the needles they would need in his lapel and wrapped suture threads around his coat buttons so they would be handy when his father needed them.

They set out shortly after sunup. Dr. Mayo urged the horses along a dirt road. Will wished his father would let him drive. Dr. Mayo always drove at a breakneck pace to reach his patients.

Cornfields stretched on both sides of the road. When the Mayos first moved to Rochester in 1864, when Will was three and before Charlie was born, most of the countryside was woods. There had been wolves and bears and Indians around then. Now they were gone.

As they approached the patient's small frame house, Will and Charlie saw buggies and wagons. They recognized the anesthetist's buggy. The patient's neighbors and family milled around in the yard or stood talking in small groups.

When he climbed down from the buggy, Dr. Mayo firmly told the people he didn't want any of them inside while he operated.

Inside, the house was clean and neat. The patient, a young woman with blond hair and dark circles under her eyes, sat in a straight chair. Charlie could tell she was frightened. He gave her an encouraging smile and forced himself not to stare at the huge lump on the right side of her abdomen.

Dr. Mayo removed his black Prince Albert coat to give himself more freedom of movement. In the kitchen, where the surgery would take place, Charlie set up the portable charcoal furnace.

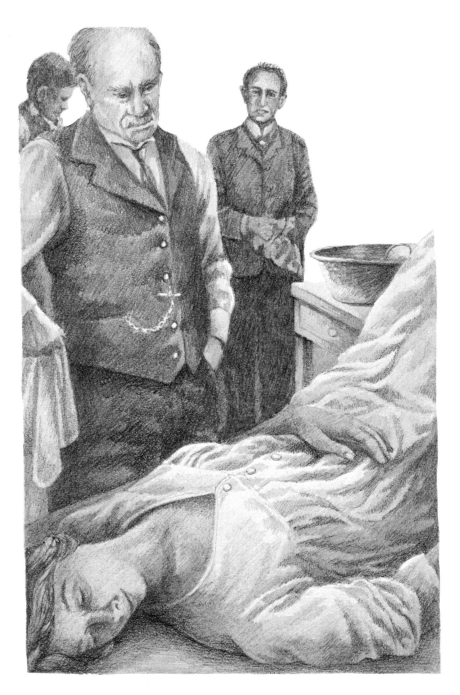

18

The furnace would heat a long piece of iron, which would be used to cauterize the wound and stop the bleeding.

The patient's husband and brother-in-law helped her onto the long kitchen table. At Dr. Mayo's direction, one of the men brought in a tin washtub and put it beside the table.

Dr. Mayo thanked the two men and asked them to join the others outside.

Charlie knew why his father didn't want them in there. Even people accustomed to the rough pioneer life on a farm were apt to faint when they saw the knife slice into flesh.

The anesthetist stood at the patient's head and began to administer chloroform. When the woman was unconscious, Charlie handed his father the knife he called for. Dr. Mayo made the incision. Will sponged up blood. Dr. Mayo inserted a trocar, a sharp-pointed instrument with three sides, into the tumor and drained its contents into the tub.

"Clamps," he said, and Charlie handed him an instrument with hooks on the end.

Dr. Mayo had drawn the design for that instrument. Using teeth from an old mowing machine for the hooks, a blacksmith had forged it for him.

Piece by piece, Dr. Mayo removed the tumor.

More than an hour had passed when it was time for Charlie to step close to his father so Dr. Mayo could reach the suturing needles and thread. Charlie was exhausted from the tension, but he had been so interested that he had hardly noticed the time.

On the way home, Charlie silently prayed that infection wouldn't set in. Even if an operation seemed successful, as this one did, postsurgical infection often killed the patient.

A week later, Will cheered when Dr. Mayo told them their patient was doing fine. Charlie couldn't cheer because of the lump in his throat. He only nodded.

Chapter Three

In September of 1880, Will went away to medical college. He didn't *choose* medicine as a career, he told friends. "I grew into it," he said, "the way a farmer's son grows into farming."

There were few good medical schools. The Mayos had decided Will should go to the University of Michigan, which had entrance requirements and promised bedside teaching.

Will's grades were not outstanding, but his practical knowledge impressed his instructors. During his last two years of the three-year course, he assisted the professor of surgery. He also won the position of assistant to the professor of anatomy.

When Dr. Will returned to Rochester, however, he had a hard time getting patients to accept him. The sick person would often say, "I want the Old Doctor" when Will responded to a call. Will would then go to tell his father that *he* was the one the patient wanted to see. But Dr. Mayo would say, "You go back and tell him I sent you." Once Will made four trips before the patient finally gave in.

Will wanted to be a surgeon, but other than amputations and ovariotomies—now called ovariectomies—there was still little surgery being performed. And Dr. Mayo thought ovariectomies were too risky for Will to attempt.

Will talked with his girlfriend, gentle, dark-haired Hattie May Damon, about his need to find a niche for himself. As they walked around the town, he wondered what he could do to help people.

Through his own pondering and observation, he found an answer. There were a lot of blind people in Rochester, and quacks selling "sight-restoring" potions took advantage of them. Many had lost their sight because of cataracts. Will had learned about cataracts at medical school, and he knew that only surgery would restore the patient's sight. But before he could operate, he needed experience. And to gain experience, he needed to practice on actual eyes.

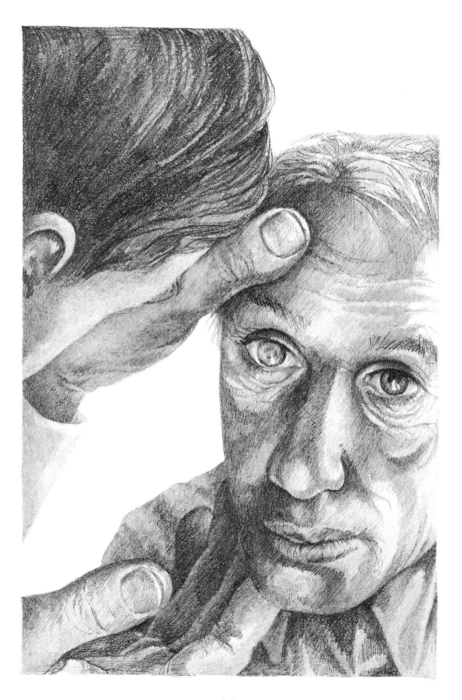

He could learn by operating on dead animals' eyes, Will decided. He set up a laboratory in a shed behind the Mayos' house. He then made trips to the slaughterhouse on the outskirts of Rochester and brought back a cow or sheep or pig's head. Charlie helped Will remove the eyes, which they studied through a magnifying glass. They cut the eyes into pieces and studied more.

Eventually, Dr. Will decided he was ready to help blind people. He went to the county poorhouse, a place for the homeless, and told two old men and an old woman with cataracts that he could remove them.

If there were a chance it would bring back their sight, they said, they were more than willing.

Dr. Will prepared carefully for the surgery. In one case, an optical nerve was nearly dead and removing the cataract did not restore sight. But the other two patients could see again, and they spread the word of the "miracle" the young doctor had performed. Soon, many people with diseases of the eye came to Dr. Will for help.

On the sweltering evening of August 21, 1883, Will and Charlie were on their way to the slaughterhouse in a phaeton, a light carriage drawn by one horse. Heavy clouds began to roll up from the horizon, but Will and Charlie weren't concerned. Rochester needed a good rain.

The brothers talked about their sister Phoebe, who had injured her spleen in 1878 when she fell from a carriage. Will and Phoebe were especially close. Although the injury had left her an invalid, Phoebe had traveled to Michigan to represent the Mayo family at Will's graduation from medical school. Since then, her condition had worsened, and no one knew how to help her.

As they drove on, the clouds became more ominous. When Will and Charlie arrived at the slaughterhouse shortly after six, the workers were leaving early. "We're in for some mean weather," old-timers told them.

Will and Charlie immediately headed back to town. A little later, the sky took on a greenish cast. Will urged the mare, Midge, to a gallop. They were almost to the Zumbro River when Charlie, looking westward, saw a funnel drop out of the clouds. The air became deathly still, and they heard a noise like the rumbling of an approaching train.

Charlie and Will were the last people to cross the Zumbro River that night. The bridge collapsed behind them. Will and Charlie managed to reach the center of town just as the tornado caught up with them. A heavy, sixteen-foot-long cornice from the top of the Cook House Hotel wall dropped on them. It broke the phaeton's shaft and knocked Midge down.

Free of the phaeton, the mare stumbled to her feet, ran down Zumbro Street, turned into an alley, and went straight to the blacksmith shop. Will and Charlie followed right behind her. Just as they reached the shop and ducked inside, its tin roof blew off. The trembling horse leaned into the wall, and so did Will and Charlie.

The wind suddenly stopped. Will and Charlie stood in the pelting rain, glad to be alive.

The tornado had killed twenty-two people and injured more than a hundred. Many of the injured went to the Buck Hotel, where Dr. Mayo was in charge; to the Mayo office, where Will and Charlie worked through the night; and to the Sisters of St. Francis convent.

The next morning, a closed dance hall, Rommell Hall, was chosen as a makeshift hospital for all the injured who still required care. Homemakers cooked meals and helped care for the injured. But they couldn't continue for long; they had their own families to take care of.

Mother Alfred and the other Sisters of St. Francis offered their services. Dr. Mayo gratefully accepted, and he and Mother Alfred soon became friends.

After the last patient went home, Mother Alfred went to see Dr. Mayo. "Rochester needs a hospital," she said.

Dr. Mayo replied that he didn't have much use for hospitals, that for the most part they were foul, dirty places.

"Our hospital, St. Mary's, will be different," she said.

Dr. Mayo argued that hospitals cost a lot of money—as much as forty thousand dollars.

Mother Alfred said they would raise that—and more if it were needed.

The sisters collected donations. They saved money by eating inexpensive food and wearing the cheapest shoes they could buy. They also took in sewing.

When Dr. Mayo realized how serious the sisters were, he withdrew his objections and began looking for a place to build the hospital.

Will was interested in the future hospital, but mostly his mind was on Hattie. He proposed to her, and on November 10, 1884, they were married.

Chapter Four

For their honeymoon, Will and Hattie spent two months in New York. While there, Dr. Will visited clinics and studied new surgical methods.

After watching a few different surgeons, he chose to observe Dr. Henry B. Sands at Roosevelt Hospital. Dr. Will got to the amphitheater every day before the surgeries began at two o'clock, and he stayed until the last one was over around seven.

Impressed by Will's interest, Dr. Sands invited him to go to a ward with him to see a patient. The man's abdomen was swollen. He was feverish, vomiting, and in great pain. "This is a case of perityphlitis," the doctor said. Dr. Will recognized it as the same, very old affliction his father called "inflammation of the bowels." Dr. Mayo had always treated it with a tonic.

Dr. Sands, however, had the patient taken to an operating room. Will watched as Dr. Sands opened the right side of the abdomen and drained off the pus. This method of treatment had saved the lives of a lot of people with perityphlitis, Dr. Sands told Will.

When Will and Hattie returned to Rochester, he described the case and Dr. Sands's surgery to his father.

Not long afterward, a young woman, a teacher, with the same symptoms as the New York patient, sent for Dr. Mayo. Dr. Will went with him.

"Inflammation of the bowels," Dr. Mayo said after he examined the patient. He prescribed the usual medicine.

"It's perityphlitis, Father," Will said. "The simple operation I told you about will save her life. Please, let me do it."

"We'll leave it to the parents to decide," Dr. Mayo said.

They refused to let Will operate. The young teacher died within hours.

Dr. Will persuaded her parents to let him do an autopsy. When he saw the abscess, his father was convinced that Will's diagnosis had been right. But what had caused the abscess?

In May of that year, 1885, Will's beloved sister Phoebe died from the injury to her spleen. Just one month later, Dr. Reginald Fitz, a pathologist, made a major surgical breakthrough. He said the *appendix* was the site of perityphlitis. He further said that an infected appendix should be totally removed. Will wondered if a similar operation of the spleen might have saved Phoebe's life. He was more determined than ever to read and study everything he could find about the body and its organs.

In the fall of the same year, Charlie enrolled in Northwestern University's medical program. Medical training was improving. He was allowed to assist in surgery at Mercy Hospital in Chicago. He spent his spare time going to other Chicago hospitals to observe.

When Charlie went home in the summer of 1886, he and Will and their father talked about the future hospital. The next summer, Dr. Mayo chose the site—nine acres outside the city limits on Zumbro Street.

In March of 1888, Charlie received his degree, and St. Mary's Hospital was nearing completion. It looked like a big, comfortable home and would have space for twenty-seven beds and an operating room. Dr. Charlie looked forward to practicing there. But in the meantime, he would work with Will and his father.

His plans dissolved when he became sick with whooping cough, a serious disease usually affecting children. Six months later, he was still thin and weak. His family decided that he should go to Europe for a rest and a change of scenery.

Charlie did have some time to rest in Europe. But since Europe was the center of medical knowledge, he wanted to learn all he could while he was there. In Paris, he attended a lecture by Louis Pasteur. Because the lecture was in French, he could understand only a few words, but he knew the talk was about bacteria—a popular and important issue among medical people. Most of the surgeons Charlie had observed in college had used antiseptics against harmful bacteria. But other reputable doctors still scorned the whole idea. The argument was far from settled.

From France, Dr. Charlie went to Germany. There he saw in the operating rooms fanatical hand washing and nail cleaning. Some surgeons wore white cloth gloves that had been boiled. Cleaning solutions were sloshed on the floor so often that the surgical team wore rubber boots.

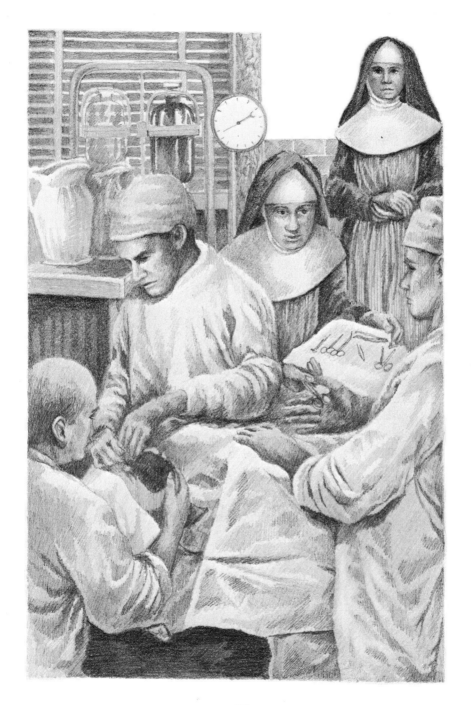

All kinds of antiseptic solutions lined the walls.

Charlie could hardly wait to get home to tell Will. Will had practically memorized a book about antisepsis. Charlie took notes so he could tell Will in detail how it was done in actual practice.

Using the wet antisepsis method, the first surgery—for cancer of the eye—took place at St. Mary's on September 30, 1889. Dr. Charlie, who Will said was better with eye surgery than he was, performed the operation. Dr. Will assisted. Their father gave the anesthetic.

The operation was successful—and there was no postsurgical infection. St. Mary's was off to a good start.

Chapter Five

Many American hospitals were more modern than St. Mary's, but St. Mary's was cleaner than most. It did have some modern conveniences, like a bell system for patients to use when they needed assistance.

The Mayo families had given the bell system to St. Mary's as a Christmas gift. Charlie and a neighbor boy installed it. Sometimes, though, it aggravated patients and staff. A bell would start ringing—and keep ringing. The only way the sisters could make it stop was to cut the wire with a big pair of scissors. The next day, Charlie would have to install it all over again.

The Mayos' offices were in the nearby Ramsey Building, but they treated the sick and performed operations at St. Mary's. They charged according to what the patient could afford. Hospital beds were a dollar per day, but if the patient couldn't pay at all, that was all right too.

When patients went home, they told friends and relatives how pleased they were with the hospital and "Mayo's clinic at St. Mary's." When these friends and relatives needed to have surgery, they, too, went to St. Mary's. Even more patients came when the Chicago and Northwestern Railway named Dr. Will its area surgeon.

Word would go by wire to the nearest train dispatcher: "Derailed passenger train. Five killed. Sixteen injured. Dr. Mayo needed at once."

A special train or a detached engine would then come at top speed to pick up Dr. Will. He sent those with serious injuries to St. Mary's.

The *Rochester Post* and the patients' hometown papers carried articles about the injured and their treatment. Back at home, released patients praised the Doctors Mayo and St. Mary's Hospital.

Times

FEBRUARY 18, 1893 VOL.

Duluth Daily Herald. Calumet

CITY OF DULUTH, SATURDAY MORNING JULY

THE MAYOS AND TH

The St. Cloud Journal-Press

ST. CLOUD, STEARNS CO. THURSDAY, MAY 13, 1895 SURGERY ADVANCES IN MAYO CLINIC

VOL. I

ST. ANTHONY AND

Paul Evening New

APOLIS, FRIDAY, OCTOBER 25, 1892

SAGA OF TWO COUNTRY BOYS IN 'BIG' MEDICINE

The Mayos of Rochester

The Rochester Post.

ROCHESTER, MINNESOTA, FRIDAY, JANUARY 12, 1892

NUMBER 12

VOLUME XL

Rochester will have important

SPECIAL TRAINS CARRY SICK TO MAYO C

— The Daily Express —

Mayo Bros E.B. Harvey and wife were among those traveling to for purpose

LOOKING FORWAR

Paris Exposition Portfolio

INTERPRETATION ME POLITICAL ING MADE.

St. Paul Dispatch

ST. PAUL, MINN., FRIDAY, JUNE 15, 1897 TWO

OCTOR'S EVIDENCE

Rationale of the Care of Chronic Catarrh.

w Permanent Cures are Made.

The order in which the symptoms of chronic catarrh occur are nearly always as follows: A cold, which hangs longer than usual; a sensitiveness assages by which one continual, set- chest; more ency, ough, his is nptoms appear ortunate ymptoms

IMPORTA RAILRO

WORLD CLINIC RESTORES HEALTH TO AILING

YEARS HENCE | BUSINESS LOCALS | ARRESTED AT ST. CLOUD

Mr Baldwin and splendid mans and a very fine feeling much better

As word spread, patients began to come from Wisconsin, Iowa, the Dakota Territory, and Nebraska. They, in turn, wrote to friends and family members in other parts of the country. More and more people came from farther and farther away.

Mother Alfred reminded Dr. Mayo and Will and Charlie that the sisters were trained as teachers—not nurses. She asked them to find someone to teach them how to care for patients.

In 1890, Edith Graham of Rochester, who had graduated from a Chicago nursing school, joined the staff to teach the sisters nursing skills. Within a few months, Miss Graham became the anesthetist at St. Mary's for the Doctors Mayo.

Charlie found it hard to concentrate when Miss Graham was around. He soon began to escort her to parties and picnics, and in April of 1893, Miss Graham became Mrs. Charles Mayo.

In what had been a frontier town when they were children, Will and Charlie now grappled with a new frontier—surgery. There were so many questions to be answered. Since tonsils caused so many problems, should they be removed as a matter of course? Would the patient survive if part of the stomach were removed? Could someone live with only one kidney?

In order to learn more, Will and Charlie took turns traveling to big cities, where they took courses and observed other surgeons. They never went away at the same time. They had made a vow that one of them would always be in Rochester.

Dr. Will's chief interest was in abdominal surgery. He had successes—and he had failures.

Abdominal surgery included operations on female organs. Although there had been much progress since the days when Dr. Mayo first removed ovarian tumors, patients still died. When that happened, Will and Charlie went over the operation step-by-step to determine what had gone wrong. By doing this, they came up with better techniques. The success rate improved, but Will felt that he was still losing too many patients.

He knew of a surgeon in Philadelphia named Dr. Joseph Price, who claimed to have a high rate of success in surgery involving women's reproductive organs. Will decided to go to Philadelphia to watch him operate.

Charlie told Will he didn't envy him that visit. According to people who knew Dr. Price, he was kind to patients, but he had a cruel, sarcastic tongue with other doctors. There were also doctors who said Dr. Price's claims were lies. Will and Charlie didn't pay much attention to such charges. They knew doctors often made them because they were jealous.

In Philadelphia, Will went three straight mornings to Dr. Price's small hospital. Each time, he was told that Dr. Price was out of town. On the fourth morning, Dr. Will was sitting in the tiny reception room when a tall man with a mustache strode in. The man bluntly asked Will who he was and what he wanted.

"I'm Dr. Will Mayo from Rochester, Minnesota, and I want to watch Dr. Price operate," Will said.

The man said he was Dr. Price and that there were already more people around than he cared to fool with. He started to walk away.

"I've waited for four days," Will said. Then, because he knew Dr. Price didn't think much of the doctors in New York, he added that he would leave and go on to New York.

Dr. Price snorted. "You won't learn anything there," he said. "Follow me." He walked ahead of Will into a poorly furnished operating room. The operating table was only a wide board laid across two sawhorses.

For three weeks, Dr. Will watched Dr. Price

work. He found that the surgeon's claims were not lies, that they weren't even exaggerated. When Will went home, he was able to save many more of his own patients. Both he and Charlie went to learn from Dr. Price in following years. And when other doctors came to observe them operate, they credited Dr. Price with their success in that field.

With his nimble, sure hands, Dr. Charlie concentrated on operations involving the eyes, nose, and throat. Dr. Will did most of the abdominal surgeries. Either brother could take over for the other, and both did operations on the arms and legs.

While they learned from other surgeons, they also invented techniques of their own. In one case, a man came in with a badly infected knee joint. Since no one knew how to drain and clean the knee's inner cavities, the accepted procedure was to amputate.

Charlie hated to do amputations, so he decided to try a radically different approach. He would cut across the knee right down to the infected area. If it worked, it would leave the man with a stiff leg, but that would be better than losing part of his leg.

Dr. Charlie made an incision from one side of the knee to the other and laid the joint wide open. He drained off the pus and packed antiseptic gauze into the cavity. To everyone's amazement, the inflammation subsided within a few hours. Charlie put the knee joint back into position, and the patient was soon up and walking around.

Dr. Charlie wrote a detailed report. It was published in the *Annals of Surgery*, the most prestigious surgical journal of the time.

Dr. Arpad Gerster of New York read the article and used Charlie's method. In an article in the same journal, Dr. Gerster attested to the worth of the "Mayo method."

Will wrote articles about abdominal surgery, and Mayo reports were published more and more often. Across the country, surgeons started to pay attention. Will and Charlie continued to learn from them, but now famous surgeons also learned from the Doctors Mayo.

Chapter Six

Dr. Charlie and Dr. Will had grown up with their father's saying, "No man is big enough to be independent of others." They had welcomed their first partner in 1892, and in 1894 they accepted a second partner. They sought out qualified doctors and scientists, and they always invited suggestions for improvement.

Medical people in big cities heard about the Mayos' team approach. Because most surgeons were individualists who liked being stars, they shook their heads. "It won't work," they said.

Dr. Will and Dr. Charlie's response was to welcome more talented people into their practice. Quarters in the Ramsey Building were no longer large enough to accommodate the growing staff, and in 1901, they moved to the old Masonic Temple.

By 1905, Dr. Will was considered the top American authority on abdominal surgery. Dr. Charlie was hailed for his successful removal of simple goiters. An affliction of the thyroid gland, simple goiters caused abnormal swelling at the front of the neck, which could interfere with the patient's breathing.

Surgeons from all over the United States, and from other countries as well, came to observe the Doctors Mayo. They read Will's and Charlie's articles and crowded into auditoriums to hear them speak.

Dr. Will became known as an exceptional speaker. He had a simple formula: Make a strong opening statement. Present your case. Keep an eye on your watch. When fifteen minutes have passed—sit down.

Dr. Charlie, on the other hand, had a hard time with speeches. "Help me rehearse, Edith," he would say.

"Play quietly," Mrs. Mayo would tell the children. "Your father has to work on his speech."

Then, she'd read the speech and suggest changes. She would critique it while Charlie practiced. But when Mrs. Mayo sat in the audience, she never heard the speech as they rehearsed it.

45

Something in the script would remind Dr. Charlie of a story, and he would wander from the notes he had prepared. He couldn't help throwing in a funny story no matter how serious the subject.

Once Dr. Charlie became comfortable with public speaking, he, too, received many requests to make talks. His warmth and humor pleased listeners. They told and retold his stories.

Dr. Will had his own kind of humor. He was a master of quick wit, especially when it came to putting the pompous in their place. One day, a rich, self-important man from another state marched into Dr. Will's office and demanded to talk to the head doctor. "I guess you're the one," he said.

"Why, no," Dr. Will said, "I'm just the belly doctor. My brother's the head doctor. He must be the one you want to see."

Not long after this incident, on March 6, 1911, sadness filled all of Rochester. Will and Charlie's father had died. Had he lived one more month, he would have been 92.

In mid-December of that same year, Dr. Charlie became sick far from home. He was in Washington, D.C., to speak to a surgical society.

Edith had made the trip East with him, but she

had stayed in New York. Dr. Charlie didn't feel well when he gave his talk, and immediately afterward, he decided to leave Washington to join Edith. By the time he reached her, he knew he had to enter a hospital. His self-diagnosis was gallstones.

The examining doctors, however, decided he had acute appendicitis and told him he must have surgery immediately.

Edith sent Dr. Will a telegram.

Dr. Will wanted to go to New York to be with Charlie, but that would mean breaking their vow that one of them would always be in Rochester. Besides, Will told himself, some of the best doctors in the country were in New York. They would take good care of Charlie.

A week later, on December 23 at around 3:30 in the morning, Dr. Will received a telephone call from Edith. "Charlie does have gallstones," she said. "He has to undergo surgery again."

This was one time, Dr. Will decided, when he had to break his and Charlie's rule. "I'm coming to do the operation," he told her. He got in touch with Miss Florence Henderson, Dr. Charlie's special anesthetist, and asked her to go with him.

The Chicago and Northwestern Railway did everything it could to get Dr. Will to New York.

It fired up a switch engine to take Will and Miss Henderson to Winona. There, a sleek new engine —and one car—were waiting for them. Dr. Will and Miss Henderson were the only passengers on a record-breaking ride to Chicago. But in Chicago, there was a delay.

The New York doctors decided they couldn't wait any longer. By the time Will and Miss Henderson arrived, the surgery was over.

Dr. Charlie was very sick after the operation. Will stayed with him through New Year's Day.

When he was well enough to travel, Dr. Charlie returned to Rochester. And the Mayo brothers went back to their commitment that one of them would always be there.

That same year, 1912, they decided to build a clinic that would put everything under one roof. Offices and laboratories had become a maze of buildings and rooms weaving around retail stores.

The redbrick building, with its cornerstone laid on the site of Will and Charlie's childhood home on Franklin Street, formally opened on March 6, 1914. It occupied a quarter of a block, had five floors, and would accommodate fourteen thousand patients per year.

Dr. Henry Plummer, a clinic partner, had

supervised the design, including the interior. Far different from the dark and gloomy Masonic Temple building, the new clinic was cheerful and spacious. Patients didn't mind waiting in a lobby graced with a fountain and ferns.

There were now five partners, and the new clinic's official name included each of their names. It was too much of a mouthful. Visiting physicians dubbed it Mayos' Clinic.

Rochester citizens shook their heads. "This time," they said, "they've gone overboard. They'll never need that much space."

Even Dr. Will and Dr. Charlie worried that the clinic building was too large. "I hope a year from now it's not going to be called 'Mayos' folly,'" Will said.

Their mother, who died the same year the clinic opened, never had those doubts. And, until her final days, she read every medical article her sons wrote. She had good reason to be proud of her sons. Their skills had helped thousands of people.

Chapter Seven

Less than a year after the clinic opened, it was clear that it was not too big—it was too small. The staff began to talk about the need for a new and larger building.

Charlie and Will talked about what to do with their money. The man they had hired to manage their funds had made such good investments they had become rich. They wanted to give the money back to the people, from whom it came. They believed that the best way to do so would be to donate a million and a half dollars to the University of Minnesota. The money would be used for generations to come for medical education and research.

Not long after they bestowed the gift, in 1917,

Germany sank an American ship. The United States declared war on Germany and entered World War I. Will and Charlie, first lieutenants in the medical reserve corps, received notices that they had been promoted. They were now majors. And, the notices said, they were needed in Washington.

The Army chiefs allowed them to take shifts in Washington so that one or the other of them could be in Rochester at all times. The one in Rochester would help conduct a training center for the Army and Navy medical corps.

Dr. Will took easily to the military. Dr. Charlie had a hard time with all the regulations. He forgot to button his coat. He misplaced one of his boot spurs and put the other one on upside down. It always surprised him when men in uniform saluted him. By the time he returned the salute, the soldier might be well past him.

When a group of medical men from England came to Rochester, they spent the night at Dr. Charlie's home. As was their custom, they left their shoes outside their bedroom doors for polishing. The war had left the Mayos with few servants—and those who remained had retired for the night. Dr. Charlie picked up a pair of shoes and took them to the kitchen. Far into the night, he was still polishing shoes.

Both brothers worked hard to organize and advise the military medical personnel in the war effort, and higher military ranks and awards followed. In July 1918, Will and Charlie were promoted to colonels, and after the war, they received Distinguished Service Crosses and were promoted to brigadier generals.

With peace restored in 1918, the Doctors Mayo looked to the future. In the mid-1920s, work began on a new Mayo Clinic. Completed, it stood fifteen stories high and had a four-story bell tower. Dedicated "to the relief of suffering humanity" on March 17, 1927, the staff began to move into the building in early 1928.

On July 1 of that year, at age 67, Dr. Will came out of the operating room at St. Mary's Hospital and went to the Clinic. He was in a depressed mood. "That was my last surgery," he told his secretary. When she asked why, he said he wanted to quit while he was still good.

"Too many surgeons continue to operate when their reactions are no longer as quick as they should be," he said.

A year and a half later, Dr. Charlie had a retinal

hemorrhage while he was operating. He was never again well. On May 26, 1939, he died while on a trip to Chicago.

Dr. Will had just discovered that he had stomach cancer. He immediately underwent surgery and seemed to rally. But within a short time, he became too weak to try anymore. He died on July 28, 1939, at the age of 78.

Because of their philosophy that people should learn, share their knowledge, and work as a team, Will and Charlie's battle against injury and disease did not end with their deaths.

Today the Mayo Clinic remains the largest private group practice in the world. It is affiliated with St. Mary's Hospital and Rochester Methodist Hospital, two of the world's largest and best-equipped hospitals.

Research to develop new medical technology continues, and people from all over the world go to the Mayo Clinic for diagnosis and treatment.

SOURCES

Clark Nelson, Mayo historian, Rochester, MN.

Dr. Samuel F. Haines, friend and associate of Drs. William James and Charles Horace Mayo.

Clapesattle, Helen. *The Doctors Mayo* (second edition). Minneapolis: University of Minnesota Press, 1975.

Johnson, Victor, M.D., Ph.D., D.Sc. *Mayo Clinic, Its Growth and Progress*. Bloomington: Voyageur Press, 1984.

Regli, Adolph. *The Mayos, Pioneers in Medicine*. New York: Julian Messner, Inc., 1942.

Webster's American Biographies. Springfield: G. & C. Merriam Company, 1974.